Psoriasis Book

Diet Plan That Healed Psoriasis Naturally

Pagano G. Anthony

Table of Contents

Psoriasis Book 1

INTRODUCTION 6

CHAPTER 1 8

What Is Psoriasis? 8

What are the various types of psoriasis? 10

What exactly are the symptoms? 13

Diagnosing psoriasis 17

Treatment plans for psoriasis 21

Coping with psoriasis 28

Psoriasis statistics 33

CHAPTER 2 36

Types of Psoriasis and Treatment Options 36

Who Will Get Psoriasis? 36

What Can Cause Psoriasis? 37

Exactly What Does Psoriasis Appear To Be? 38

Is Psoriasis Curable? 42

Treatment - Topical Agents 45

What's the Long-Term Prognosis in Patients With
Psoriasis?... 47

CHAPTER 3.. 49

6 Ways to Cover Your Psoriasis 49

CHAPTER 4.. 53

Twelve home cures for treating Psoriasis 53

CHAPTER 5.. 73

Psoriasis Dos and Don'ts 73

Psoriasis Dos 74

Psoriasis Don'ts 79

CHAPTER 6.. 82

7 Methods for Psoriasis Skin Care........................... 82

CHAPTER 7..89

Risks of Not Treating Psoriasis..................................89

Physical risks..90

Reduced standard of living 92

Depression, anxiety, and suicide 93

Various other inflammatory conditions..................94

Not only skin deep 95

A c k n o w l e d g m e n t s 96

INTRODUCTION

Psoriasis is a persistent autoimmune skin condition, which isn't contagious. Psoriasis affects both skins as well as the joints of an average person who is suffering from the disease. Psoriasis typically causes your skin to be red and scaly.

Ensuring that your skin is healthy and look beautiful is not an easy task, without obtaining a skin disease such as psoriasis to make things worse. There is nothing easy about coping with this autoimmune skin condition, which is particularly challenging because you never know if it is likely to flare up. This type of unpredictability can adversely influence many regions of your life and may affect you emotionally, wreaking havoc on your sense of self-esteem. Psoriasis often ends up affecting how you dress, how you behave and relate with other people, also to some extent, even how you perform your activities at work. Since psoriasis can destroy self-confidence, there is no limit to the quantity of damage it could do in your daily life.

This book will let you know the reality from research and testing of different natural essential products for psoriasis and demonstrate everything you can eat to improve your life, remove psoriasis, and start exercise routine you always imagined. You'll need to relax before you start meditating, and handle any stress that comes to your path. Be familiar with how to be at rest 24 hours a day, in hectic surroundings, while keeping your family healthy and happy. You need to see the reality of Psoriasis. You will need this book as a foundation for the next fantastic chapter in life.

When you have psoriasis, this book can transform all of your viewpoint of the disease and why it is in your daily life."

CHAPTER 1

What Is Psoriasis?

Based on a series of medical research, Psoriasis is well known to be a chronic ailment that triggers the rapid buildup of skin cells. There is a high tendency of scaling surfacing on the surface of the skin due to the buildup of cells. Seeing that there are redness and inflammation around the scales are things that are so common. Typical psoriatic scales are developed in thick, red, and whitish-silver patches. Sometimes, these patches will bleed after been cracked.

Psoriasis may be the consequence of a sped-up skin production process. Typically, skin cells grow deep in your skin and slowly rise to the top. Eventually, they fall off. The normal life cycle of the skin cell is a month.

In people who have psoriasis, this production process might occur in a few days. As a result of this, no one knows when the skin cells fall off. This rapid overproduction leads to the buildup or increase of skin cells.

Scales typically develop on joints, such as elbows, and legs. They could develop anywhere on your body, like the:

- Hands

- Feet

- Neck

- Scalp

- Face

Psoriasis that are not common affect the nails, the mouth,

and the region around genitals. According to one examination, 7.4 million Americans have psoriasis. It's commonly connected with several other circumstances, including:

- Type 2 diabetes

- Inflammatory colon disease

- Heart disease

- Psoriatic arthritis

- Anxiety

- Depression

What are the various types of psoriasis?

You can find five types of psoriasis:

Plaque psoriasis

Plaque psoriasis may be the most common type of psoriasis. The American Academy of Dermatology

10

(AAD) estimates that about 80 percent of individuals with the problem have plaque psoriasis. It causes red, inflamed patches that cover regions of your skin. These patches tend to be covered with whitish-silver scales or plaques. These plaques are generally on the elbows, legs, and scalp.

Guttate psoriasis

Guttate psoriasis is common in childhood. This sort of psoriasis causes small pink areas. The most frequent sites for guttate psoriasis are the torso, arms, and legs. The major observable thing is that the spots are rarely thick or raised like plaque psoriasis.

Pustular psoriasis

Pustular psoriasis is more prevalent in adults. It causes white, pus-filled blisters and broad regions of red, inflamed skin. Pustular psoriasis is normally localized to smaller parts of the body, like the hands or feet.

Nonetheless, it can be common.

Inverse psoriasis

Inverse psoriasis causes bright regions of red, shiny, inflamed skin. Patches of inverse psoriasis develop under armpits or breasts, in the groin, or about skinfolds in the genitals.

Erythrodermic psoriasis

Erythrodermic psoriasis is a severe and incredibly rare kind of psoriasis. This form often covers large parts of the body simultaneously. Your skin almost appears sunburned. Scales that often develop slough off in large sections or sheets. It's not unusual for anybody with this sort of psoriasis to have a fever or become very ill.

This type could be life-threatening, so individuals should see a medical expert immediately.

What exactly are the symptoms?

Psoriasis symptoms change from individual to individual and depend on the sort of psoriasis. Regions of psoriasis are often as small as a few flakes over the scalp or elbow or cover a lot of the body.

The most frequent symptoms of plaque psoriasis include:

- Red, Raised, Inflamed Patches Of Skin

- Whitish-Silver Scales Or Plaques Around The Red Patches

- Dry Skin That May Crack And Bleed

- Soreness Around Patches

- Itching And Burning Sensations Around Patches

- Thick, Pitted Nails

- Unpleasant, Swollen Joints

Don't assume that everybody will experience many of

these symptoms. Some individuals will experience entirely different symptoms if indeed they have a less common kind of psoriasis.

A lot of people with psoriasis go through "cycles" of symptoms. The problem could cause severe symptoms for a couple of days or weeks when not quickly attended to, and the symptoms may get rid of and become almost unnoticeable. Then, in a couple of weeks or if compounded with a common psoriasis trigger, the problem may flare up again. Sometimes, symptoms of psoriasis disappear completely.

When you have no active signs of the problem, you might be in "remission." That doesn't mean psoriasis won't keep coming back, but for now, you're symptom-free.

Is psoriasis contagious?

Psoriasis isn't contagious. You can't transfer your skin ailment from one person to another. Touching a psoriatic lesion on someone else won't make you develop the problem. You must be educated on the problem, as many people think psoriasis is contagious.

What can cause psoriasis?

Doctors are unclear in regards to what causes psoriasis. However, because of years of research, they have an over-all notion of two key factors: genetics as well as the immune system.

Immune system

Psoriasis can be an autoimmune condition. Autoimmune conditions will be the consequence of your body attacking itself. Regarding psoriasis, white blood cells referred to as T cells mistakenly attack your skin cells.

15

In an average body, white blood cells are deployed to attack and destroy invading bacteria and fight infections. This mistaken attack causes your skin cell production process to get into overdrive. The sped-up skin cell production causes new skin cells to build up too quickly. They may be pushed towards the skin's surface, where they accumulate.

This leads to the plaques that are mostly connected with psoriasis. The attacks on your skin cells also cause red, inflamed regions of skin to build up.

Genetics

Some individuals inherit genes that make them much more likely to build up psoriasis. When you have an immediate relative with your skin condition, your risk for developing psoriasis is higher. However, the percentage of individuals who've psoriasis and a genetic predisposition is small. Approximately 2-3 percent of individuals using the gene develop the problem, based on the National Psoriasis Foundation (NPF).

Diagnosing psoriasis

Two tests or examinations could be essential to diagnose psoriasis.

Physical examination

Most doctors can produce a diagnosis with a straightforward physical exam. Symptoms of psoriasis are usually apparent and easy to tell apart from other circumstances that could cause similar symptoms. In this exam, make sure you explain things to your doctor explicitly every area of concern. Furthermore, let your physician know if any family has the problem.

Biopsy

If the symptoms are unclear or if your physician wants to confirm their suspected diagnosis, they could have a small sample of skin. That is referred to as a biopsy.

You will be taken to a lab, where the health care practitioners will have to examined your skin under a microscope. The examination can diagnose the sort of psoriasis you possess. Additionally, it may rule out various other possible disorders or infections.

Most biopsies are done in your doctor's office on the day of your appointment. Your physician will probably inject an area numbing medication to help make the biopsy less painful. They'll then send the biopsy to a lab for analysis.

When the results return, your physician may request a scheduled appointment to go over the findings and treatment plans with you.

Psoriasis triggers: Stress, alcohol, and more

External "triggers" may begin with a new episode of psoriasis. These triggers aren't the same for everybody. They could also change as time passes for you.

The most frequent triggers for psoriasis include:

- Stress

Unusually high stress may trigger a flare-up. If you figure out how to reduce and manage your stress, you can reduce and perhaps prevent flare-ups.

- Alcohol

Heavy use of alcohol can trigger psoriasis flare-ups. If you excessively use alcohol, psoriasis outbreaks could be even more frequent. Reducing alcohol consumption makes sense for a lot more than your skin layer too. Your physician might help you shape a plan to give up drinking if you want help.

- Injury

A major accident, cut, or scrape may trigger a flare-up. Shots, vaccines, and sunburns may also trigger a fresh outbreak.

- Medications

Some medications are believed to triggers psoriasis. These medications include:

- lithium

- antimalarial medications

- high blood circulation pressure medication

- Infection

Psoriasis is caused, at least partly, by the disease fighting capability mistakenly attacking healthy skin cells. If you're sick or battling with an infection, your disease fighting capability will get into overdrive to fight chlamydia. This might result in another psoriasis flare-up. Strep throat can be a common trigger.

Treatment plans for psoriasis

Psoriasis does not have any cure. Treatments try to reduce inflammation and scales, likewise slow the growth of skin cells, and remove plaques.

Topical treatments

Ointments and creams applied right to your skin are a good idea for reducing mild to moderate psoriasis.

Topical psoriasis treatments include:

- Topical corticosteroids

- Topical retinoids

- Anthralin

- Vitamin d analogues

- Salicylic acid

- Moisturizer

Systemic medications

People who have moderate to severe psoriasis, and the ones who haven't responded good to additional treatment types might need to use oral or injected medications. Several medications have severe unwanted effects. Doctors usually prescribe them for short intervals.

These medications include:

- Methotrexate

- Cyclosporine (sandimmune)

- Biologics

- Retinoids

Light therapy

This psoriasis treatment uses ultraviolet (UV) or daylight. Sunlight kills the overactive white blood cells that are attacking healthy skin cells and causing rapid cell growth. Both UVA and UVB light could help reduce symptoms of mild to moderate psoriasis.

A lot of people with moderate to severe psoriasis will reap the benefits of a combined mix of treatments. This sort of therapy uses several procedures to lessen symptoms. Some individuals could use the same treatment for their entire lives. Others might need to change treatments occasionally if their skin stops responding to what they're using.

Medication for psoriasis

When you have average to severe psoriasis - or if psoriasis stops responding to other treatments - your physician may consider an oral or injected medication.

The most frequent oral and injected medications used to take care of psoriasis include:

Biologics

This class of medications alters your disease fighting capability and prevents interactions in the middle of your disease, fighting capability and inflammatory pathways. These medications are injected or given through intravenous (IV) infusion.

Retinoids

Retinoids reduce skin cell production. Once you stop using them, symptoms of psoriasis will probably return. Unwanted effects include hair thinning and lip inflammation.

People who are pregnant or could become pregnant in next three years shouldn't take retinoids due to the chance of possible congenital disabilities.

Cyclosporine

Cyclosporine (Sandimmune) prevents the immune system's response. This may ease symptoms of psoriasis. Also, it means you have a weakened disease fighting capability so that you might be sick easily. Side effects consist of kidney problems and high blood circulation pressure.

Methotrexate

Like cyclosporine, methotrexate suppresses the disease fighting capability. It could cause fewer unwanted effects when found in low doses. Serious unwanted effects consist of liver damage and reduced production of red and white blood cells.

Diet tips for people who have psoriasis

Food can't cure and even treat psoriasis, but feeding on a better diet might lessen your symptoms. These five changes in lifestyle can help ease symptoms of psoriasis and reduce flare-ups:

- Lose weight

If you're overweight, slimming down may decrease the condition's severity. Slimming down may also help treat far better. It's unclear how weight interacts with psoriasis, so even in case, your symptoms remain unchanged, slimming down continues to be good for your current health.

- Eat a heart-healthy diet

Lessen your intake of fats. They are in animal products like meats and dairy. Boost your consumption of lean proteins that contain omega-3 essential fatty acids, such as salmon, sardines, and shrimp. Plant resources of omega-3s include walnuts, flax seeds, and soybeans.

- Avoid trigger foods

Psoriasis causes inflammation. Some foods cause inflammation too. Avoiding those foods might improve symptoms. These food types include:

- Red meat

- Refined sugar

- Processed foods

- Dairy products

- Drink less alcohol

Alcohol consumption can boost your risks of the flare-up. Scale back or quit entirely. When you have a problem with your alcohol, make sure that you consult your doctor to help you for a cure plan.

- Consider taking vitamins

Some doctors prefer a vitamin-rich diet to vitamins in pill form. However, even the healthiest eater might need support getting adequate nutrients. Ask your physician if you're taking any vitamins being a supplement to your daily diet.

Coping with psoriasis

Life with psoriasis could be challenging, but with the proper approach, you can reduce flare-ups and live a wholesome, fulfilling life. These three areas can help you cope in the short- and long-term:

28

- Diet

Slimming down and maintaining a healthy diet plan can go quite a long way in helping you to ease and reduce symptoms of psoriasis. This consists of eating a diet plan abundant with omega-3 essential fatty acids, whole grains, and plants. It's also advisable to limit foods that may boost your inflammation. These food types include processed sugars, milk products, and processed food items.

There is anecdotal evidence that eating nightshade fruits & vegetables can trigger psoriasis symptoms. Nightshade vegetables & fruits include tomatoes as well as white potatoes, eggplants, and pepper-derived foods like paprika and cayenne pepper (however, not black pepper, which originates from a different plant altogether).

- Stress

Stress is a well-established trigger for psoriasis. Understanding how to manage and cope with stress can help you reduce flare-ups and ease symptoms. Try the following to lessen your stress:

- Meditation

- Journaling

- Breathing

- Yoga

- Emotional health

People who have psoriasis will experience depression and self-esteem issues. You might look less confident when new spots appear. Talking with family about how psoriasis affects you might be difficult. The constant cycle of the problem could be frustrating too.

Many of these emotional issues are valid. You must look for a resource for handling them. This might include talking to a specialist mental health expert or joining an organization for those who have psoriasis.

- Psoriasis and arthritis

Between 30 and 33 percent of individuals with psoriasis will get a diagnosis of psoriatic arthritis, according to recent clinical guidelines from your AAD as well as the NPF.

This sort of arthritis causes swelling, pain, and inflammation in affected joints. It's commonly recognized incorrectly as arthritis rheumatoid or gout. The current presence of inflamed, red regions of skin with plaques usually distinguishes this sort of arthritis from others.

Psoriatic arthritis is normally a chronic condition. Like psoriasis, the symptoms of psoriatic arthritis will come and go, alternating between flare-ups and remission. Psoriatic arthritis may also be continuous, with constant symptoms and issues. This problem typically affects joints in the fingers or toes. It could also affect your back, wrists, knees, or ankles.

A lot of people who develop psoriatic arthritis have psoriasis. However, it's possible to build up the joint condition with no psoriasis diagnosis. A lot of people who receive an arthritis diagnosis with no psoriasis have a member of the family who does experience your skin condition.

Treatments for psoriatic arthritis may successfully ease

symptoms, decrease pain, and improve joint mobility. Much like psoriasis, slimming down, maintaining a healthy diet plan, and avoiding triggers also may help reduce psoriatic arthritis flare-ups. An early diagnosis and treatment solution can decrease the probability of severe complications, including joint damage.

Psoriasis statistics

Around 7.4 million people in America have psoriasis. At any age you can have psoriasis, but most diagnoses occur in adulthood. The common age of onset is between 15 to 35 years of age. Based on the World Health Organization (WHO), some studies estimate that about 75 percent of psoriasis cases are diagnosed before age 46. Another peak amount of diagnoses can happen in the late 50s and early 60s.

According to WHO, men and women are affected equally. White people are affected disproportionately. People of color constitute an extremely small proportion of psoriasis diagnoses.

Having a member of the family with the problem increases your risk for developing psoriasis. However, many people who have the condition don't have any genealogy at all. Some individuals with a family group history won't develop psoriasis.

One-third of individuals with psoriasis will be identified as having psoriatic arthritis. Furthermore, people who have psoriasis will develop circumstances such as:

- Type 2 diabetes

- Kidney disease

- Heart disease

- High blood circulation pressure

Although data isn't complete, research suggests cases of psoriasis have become more prevalent. Whether that's because people are developing the look of their skin condition or doctors are simply improving at diagnosing is unclear.

CHAPTER 2

Types of Psoriasis and Treatment Options

Psoriasis can be an autoimmune disorder where rapid skin cell reproduction leads to raised, red, and scaly patches of skin. It isn't contagious. It most often affects your skin on the elbows, legs, and scalp, though it can appear anywhere on the body.

Who Will Get Psoriasis?

Anyone can have Psoriasis. About 7.5 million people in the U.S. are affected, and it occurs equally in women and men. Psoriasis may appear at any age but is positively frequently diagnosed between the ages of 15 to 25. It is even more frequent in Caucasians.

Psoriasis is a non-curable, chronic condition of the skin, and you will see periods in which the condition will improve, and other occasions, it is going to get worse. The symptoms can range from mild, small, faint dry skin patches in which a person might not suspect they have a skin ailment to severe Psoriasis in which a person's entire body may be covered with thick, red, scaly skin plaques.

What Can Cause Psoriasis?

The reason for Psoriasis is unknown, but several risk factors are suspected. There appears to be a genetic predisposition to inheriting the condition, as Psoriasis is often within the family. Environmental factors may play a role in the disease fighting capability. The triggers for Psoriasis - what can cause people to develop it - remain unknown.

Exactly What Does Psoriasis Appear To Be?

Psoriasis usually appears as red or pink plaques of raised, thick, scaly skin. Nonetheless, it may also appear as small flat bumps or large thick plaques. It mostly affects your skin in the elbows, legs, and scalp, though it could appear anywhere on your body.

Psoriasis Vulgaris

The most frequent type of Psoriasis that affects about 80% of most sufferers is psoriasis vulgaris ("vulgaris" means common). Additionally, it is known as plaque psoriasis due to the well-defined regions of raised red skin that characterize this form. These raised red plaques have a flaky, silver-white buildup at the top called scale, composed of dead skin cells. The scale loosens and sheds frequently.

Guttate Psoriasis

Psoriasis, which has small, salmon-pink coloured drops on your skin, is guttate Psoriasis, affecting about 10% of individuals with Psoriasis. There is generally an excellent silver-white buildup (scale) over the drop-like lesion that's finer compared to the level in plaque psoriasis. This sort of Psoriasis if commonly triggered with a streptococcal (bacterial) infection. About 2-3 weeks following a bout of strep throat, a person's lesions may erupt. This outbreak can go away and may never recur.

Inverse Psoriasis

Inverse psoriasis (also known as intertriginous psoriasis) appears as red lesions in the body, mostly beneath the breasts, in the armpits, close to the genitals, beneath the buttocks, or in abdominal folds. Sweat and skin rubbing together irritate these inflamed areas.

Pustular Psoriasis

Pustular Psoriasis includes well-defined, white pustules around the skin. They are filled up with pus that is ordinarily non-infectious. Your skin bumps will be reddish, and large portions from the skin may redden too. It may follow a cycle of redness from the skin, accompanied by pustules and scaling.

Erythrodermic Psoriasis

Erythrodermic Psoriasis is certainly a rare kind of Psoriasis that's extremely inflammatory and will affect the body's surface, causing your skin to become scarlet. It seems to be red, peeling rash that often itches or burns.

Psoriasis from the Scalp

Psoriasis commonly occurs within the scalp, which might cause fine, scaly skin or heavily crusted plaque areas. This plaque may flake or peel from the lime in clumps.

Scalp psoriasis may resemble seborrheic dermatitis, however, in that condition, the scales are greasy.

Psoriatic Arthritis

Psoriatic arthritis is usually a kind of arthritis (inflammation from the joints) accompanied by inflammation of your skin (Psoriasis). Psoriatic arthritis can be an autoimmune disorder where the body's defences attack the joints of your body, causing inflammation and pain. Psoriatic arthritis usually develops about 5 to 12 years after Psoriasis starts and about 5-10% of individuals with Psoriasis will experience psoriatic arthritis.

Can Psoriasis Affect Only My Nails?

In some instances, Psoriasis may involve only the fingernails and toenails, though additionally, nail symptoms will accompany psoriasis and arthritis symptoms. The looks of the nails could be altered, and affected nails may have small pinpoint pits or large yellow-coloured separations on the nail dish called "oil spots." Nail psoriasis could be hard to take care of but may react to medications taken for psoriasis or psoriatic arthritis. Treatments include topical steroids put on the cuticle, steroid injections at the cuticle, or oral medicaments.

Is Psoriasis Curable?

There is no cure for Psoriasis. The condition can proceed into remission, where there are no symptoms or signs present. Current research is underway for better treatments and a possible cure.

Is Psoriasis Contagious?

Psoriasis isn't contagious despite having skin-to-skin

contact. It is not possible for you to catch it from touching anyone who has it, nor is it possible to pass it to anyone else when you have it.

Is it possible for me to pass psoriasis to my children?

Psoriasis could be tranfered from parents to children, as there's a genetic element of the condition. Psoriasis will run in families, and frequently, this genealogy is helpful to make a diagnosis.

The Type Of Doctors that Treats Psoriasis?

There are many types of doctors who may treat Psoriasis. Dermatologists focus on the diagnosis and treatment of Psoriasis. Rheumatologists focus on treating joint disorders, including psoriatic arthritis. Family physicians, internal medical physicians, rheumatologists, dermatologists, and other physicians may all be engaged in the care and treatment of patients with Psoriasis.

House Treatment for Psoriasis

There are few home remedies that might help minimize outbreaks or reduce symptoms of Psoriasis:

- Contact with sunlight.

- Apply moisturizers after bathing to keep skin soft.

- Avoid irritating cosmetics or soaps.

- Usually, do not scratch the area because it might lead to bleeding or excessive irritation.

- Over-the-counter cortisone creams can reduce itching of mild Psoriasis.

- A dermatologist may prescribe an ultraviolet B unit and instruct the individual at home to make use of.

Treatment - Topical Agents

The first type of treatment for Psoriasis includes topical medications put on the skin. The primary topical treatments are corticosteroids (cortisone creams, gels, liquids, sprays, or ointments), vitamin D-3 derivatives, coal tar, anthralin, or retinoids. These drugs may lose potency as time passes, so often they may be rotated or combined. Ask your doctor before combining medications, as some drugs shouldn't be combined.

Treatment - Phototherapy (Light Therapy)

Ultraviolet (UV) light from sunlight slows the production of skin cells and reduces inflammation and may lessen psoriasis symptoms in few people, and artificial light therapy can be used for other people. Sunlamps and tanning booths aren't proper substitutes for medical light sources. You will find two main types of light therapy:

- Ultraviolet B (UV-B) light therapy is usually coupled with topical treatments and works well for treating moderate-to-severe plaque psoriasis. There's a threat of skin cancer, just like there is certainly from natural sunlight.

- PUVA therapy combines an orally administered psoralen drug, which makes your skin more sensitive to light as well as the sun, with ultraviolet A (UV-A) light therapy. 85% of patients report relief of disease symptoms with 20-30 treatments. Therapy is usually given 2-3 times each week with an outpatient basis, with maintenance treatments every 2-4 weeks until remission. Nausea, itching, and burning are unwanted effects. Complications include sensitivity towards the sun, sunburn, skin cancer, and cataracts.

Treatment - Systemic Agents (Drugs Taken In the body)

If localized treatment and phototherapy have already been tried and also have failed, treatment for Psoriasis includes systemic drugs taken either orally or by injection. Drugs including methotrexate, adalimumab (Humira), ustekinumab (Stelara), secukinumab (Cosentyx), ixekizumab (Taltz), and infliximab (Remicade) block inflammation to greatly help slow skin cell growth. Systemic drugs could be recommended for those who have Psoriasis that's disabling in virtually any physical, psychological, social, or economic way.

What's the Long-Term Prognosis in Patients With Psoriasis?

The prognosis for patients with Psoriasis is good. Although the condition is chronic and isn't curable, it could be controlled effectively often.

CHAPTER 3

6 Ways to Cover Your Psoriasis

When you have Psoriasis, the discomfort of red patches and dry, cracked skin may not be the thing you're contending with: Many people are self-conscious about how their skin looks.

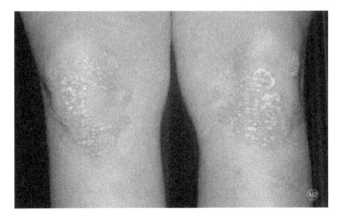

Listed below are six methods to minimize the looks of Psoriasis.

1. Observe doctor's orders

Minimize flare-ups by avoiding your psoriasis triggers.

Frequently occurring ones consist of alcohol, stress, and particular foods. Always ensure to follow your treatment solution cautiously.

2. Remove scaling

Whenever you are having a warm bath, gently rub the psoriasis plaques having a loofah sponge to loosen scaling. You may even want to use gentle cleansers containing salicylic acids to greatly help remove scaling, which not merely makes the plaque less noticeable but helps your skin layer absorb moisturizer and skin medications.

3. Moisturize your skin layer

Psoriasis patches are less noticeable when you have them moist. Ask your dermatologist for recommendations that are effective and safe to work with. In general, search for "fragrance-free," "hypoallergenic," and "non-comedogenic" (nonclogging) on product labels.

4. Camouflage it

Your dermatologist can provide you with tips for lightweight or heavyweight foundations (based on your coverage needs) that are safe to use on sensitive skin. She or he could also offer ideas for color correcting makeup (yellow- or green-based shades) if your skin layer is red. To eliminate makeup, the National Psoriasis Foundation suggests utilizing a petroleum-based remover.

5. Help to make a 'joint' effort

If you're covering up patches on joints with makeup, bend (not extend) before you apply, based on the National Psoriasis Foundation. This will prevent products from splitting up as you move. An instant spritz of waterproof hairspray might help set the building blocks on your body.

6. Hide with clothing

Based on where your plaques can be found, and the

elements, lengthy sleeves, and lengthy pants might help conceal your Psoriasis. Maintain clothing loose, so that it doesn't irritate plaques.

7. Avoid allowing it to rule your daily life

Psoriasis is something you have, not who you are. While there are occasions it might be embarrassing or cause you to feel self-conscious, make sure it doesn't affect how your home is your life.

CHAPTER 4

Twelve home cures for treating

Psoriasis

Psoriasis is a lifelong autoimmune condition of the skin where the disease fighting capability triggers the overproduction of skin cells. Some home cures can help relieve symptoms.

Psoriasis causes red, scaly patches of skin called plaques. Plaques usually appear on the elbows, knees, and scalp, however, they can form anywhere on your body.

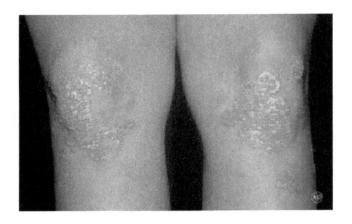

Before using home cures, it might be smart to speak to a health care practisioner. Home remedies tend to work best when people utilize them alongside treatment.

Home remedies

Using home cures, either alone or in conjunction with treatment may improve psoriasis symptoms.

However, some home cures may connect to medications, so anyone who's considering using some of them should speak to a doctor first. Additionally you must monitor psoriasis symptoms to make sure that the remedies aren't making these to get worse.

1. Contact with sunlight

Contact with sunlight will often enhance the appearance of your skin whenever a person has Psoriasis. People should expose their skin gradually as well as for brief periods. The National Psoriasis Foundation recommends you start with 5 to ten minutes of midday sun exposure once a day.

It is vital to protect healthy skin with sunscreen and clothing so that just the affected areas get contact with sunlight. If their skin tolerates it, a person might slowly increase sun exposure in increments of 30 seconds every day.

If a person gets sunburnt, they ought to avoid too much exposure to the sun. They also need to talk to a health care practisioner because sunburn could make Psoriasis worse.

It's the sun's UVB rays that are advantageous for psoriasis symptoms as opposed to the UVA rays. Sun and indoor tanning beds mostly emit UVA rays.

People who use indoor tanning beds have an increased possibility of skin damage. With them may also greatly increase the chance of a kind of skin cancer called melanoma by 59%.

Many experts, like the National Psoriasis Foundation as well as the American Academy of Dermatology, usually do not recommend the use of commercial tanning beds.

Some medications may also make your skin more sensitive to sunlight.

People should ask their doctor before trying sun exposure

being a home remedy. Individuals with a family group history of skin cancer might need to stay away from the sun and seek other treatments.

2. Fish oil or omega-3 fats

Research shows that omega-3 essential fatty acids, which fish and fish oil supplements often contain, can reduce inflammation and improve autoimmune diseases.

A 2014 meta-analysis found "moderate evidence" that fish oils will help people who have Psoriasis, which is both inflammatory and autoimmune.

However, the extent of the benefit may depend on the sort of fish oil, the dosage, and the kind of Psoriasis.

Omega-3 essential fatty acids look like the very best element of the oil. It's possible that some individuals may experience unwanted effects when working with fish oil. Potential adverse effects include:

- Nausea

- Indigestion

- Diarrhea

- A fishy taste in the mouth

Individuals who take blood thinners, such as warfarin (Coumadin), have an increased threat of bleeding if indeed they also take omega-3 supplements.

People should follow dosage instructions carefully to avoid possible stomach discomfort. As fish oil supplements can connect to some medications, people should speak to a health care provider before taking them. Ideally, it is best to take fish that contain omega-3 instead of taking supplements. Omega-3 supplements are accessible to get online.

3. Capsaicin

Capsaicin is an element of red peppers, and they have demonstrated the capability to fight inflammation. Even though the following types of experimental research are relatively old, they are the newest studies in this field. Both display that capsaicin can improve psoriasis symptoms.

In 1986, in a report that featured in the Journal from the American Academy of Dermatology, 44 people who have moderate-to-severe symptoms applied a topical capsaicin cream for six weeks.

Nearly half of the group noted burning, stinging, itching, and redness when they first apply the cream, but this stopped or vastly decreased after they continued utilizing it. The researchers suggested that capsaicin may be a good treatment for Psoriasis.

In 1993, another study investigated the usage of substance P, an element of capsaicin, for pruritic Psoriasis. The 98 participants who used the cream four times per day for six weeks reported more significant improvements in skin thickness, scaling, redness, and itching than those in the placebo group.

However, some participants reported unwanted effects, including a stinging sensation in the region where they applied the cream. Capsaicin creams can be found online as well as with pharmacies and health food stores.

4. Probiotics

Probiotics are helpful bacteria that can be found in yogurt

and fermented foods. People may also consume them in supplements.

Having the correct balance of bacteria in the torso can help the disease fighting capability. Psoriasis can be an autoimmune disease, so probiotics could help manage symptoms.

Research shows that a particular kind of probiotic called Bifidobacterium infantis 35624 can help regulate inflammatory replies in the torso that donate to psoriasis symptoms.

5. Curcumin

Curcumin may be the active component in the spice turmeric. It could lessen inflammation in the torso, and it could also reduce psoriatic activity. The findings of the 2016 report in mice led researchers to summarize that curcumin has "great potential to take care of psoriasis."

Curcumin is available online or to get in pill or capsule form.

6. Oregon grape

Oregon grape, or Mahonia aquifolium, can be an herbal remedy that might help calm the immune response in Psoriasis. In a written report on three clinical trials involving a complete 104 people, the authors conclude that M. aquifolium cream is an "effective and safe" treatment for mild-to-moderate Psoriasis.

In 2018, authors reviewing the data to aid treating Psoriasis with M. aquifolium found seven studies investigating its use. They figured M. aquifolium could improve symptoms, and it is effective and safe with few unwanted effects.

7. Aloe vera

Traditional medicine has long used the gel in the aloe vera plant to take care of skin wounds. Applying an ointment containing aloe vera also may help reduce the inflammation, scaling, and inflammation that psoriasis causes.

A 2018 study, where 2,248 people who have mild-to-moderate Psoriasis used an ointment containing either 50 percent propolis and 3 percent aloe vera or a placebo, suggested that aloe vera may be ideal for people who have this condition.

Those that used the supplements containing aloe vera experienced a "noteworthy improvement" in their symptoms.

However, before this, the American Academy of

Dermatology (AAD) noted that only two randomized placebo-controlled trials had viewed the result of aloe vera for treating Psoriasis. One showed that it had been helpful, as the various other showed it had no effect.

People should apply aloe vera right to their skin and prevent taking it internally.

The National Psoriasis Foundation recommends choosing a cream or gel which has at least 0.5 percent aloe. Many health food stores carry aloe lotions that are also open for purchase online.

8. Apple cider vinegar

Anecdotal evidence shows that apple cider vinegar will help soothe itching and burning caused by scalp psoriasis. However, it is usually not ideal for applying it to regions of broken or cracked skin. It includes natural germ-killing properties and may end up being soothing for the scalp.

For any gentler treatment, an individual can dilute the vinegar with the same amount of water. If it burns during or after application, it is advisable to stop utilizing it. There will not seem to be any scientific evidence to aid the usage of apple cider vinegar for Psoriasis.

9. Moisturizers

Itching and flaking could make Psoriasis appear and feel worse so that it is vital to maintain skin moisturized. The AAD remembers that moisturizing creams, or emollients, certainly are a standard treatment to use alongside additional therapies.

Applying much ointment or thick cream three times a day can help control symptoms and keep skin feeling comfortable. People should search for products that are free from fragrances and dyes using the label "for sensitive skin." A cream that has aloe vera can help.

Moisturizers that are ideal for people who have Psoriasis are for sale to purchase online. Doctors could also recommend topical treatments and creams containing coal tar, salicylic acid, and other medicinal ingredients.

10. Wet dressings and warm baths with salts or oats

Baths and showers could be relaxing, but the ones that are too hot can strip your skin of its oils, which could make Psoriasis worse. Some individuals find a warm bath containing colloidal oatmeal or Epsom salts is soothing and relieves symptoms.

According to analysis, an oatmeal bath or a wet dressing

can reduce itching, and a warm bath containing the right bath oil might help moisturize your skin.

In 2005, researchers found evidence that Dead Sea salts will help with dry skin. Volunteers immersed a forearm in water, having a 5-percent concentration of magnesium salts, the most frequent nutrients in the Dead Sea, for quarter-hour.

The participants' skin barrier function improved, their skin hydration was better, plus they had reduced roughness and inflammation weighed against the control group who used plain tap water instead. After bathing, applying a proper moisturizer as the skin continues to be damp might help prevent moisture loss.

11. Diet and exercise

Some individuals with Psoriasis could be more likely to become overweight and also have a greater risk of various other conditions, such as cardiovascular disease and type 2 diabetes. Exercise might help lower the chance of additional problems.

Diet can be vital in maintaining a wholesome weight and avoiding cardiovascular and other styles of disease.

Tips that might help include:

- Avoiding sugar

- Drinking a lot of water

- Eliminating trans fats, which can be found in lots of fast and processed food items

- Eating foodstuffs with anti-inflammatory properties, including many vegetables & fruits

12. Additional alternative therapies

Other home cures that people have tested include:

- Acupressure

- Acupuncture

- Massage

- Reiki

- Yoga or tai chi

There is no evidence that these can specifically benefit a person with Psoriasis. However, acupuncture and massage might help relieve pain, plus they may be good for anyone who has psoriatic arthritis.

People should talk with their doctor before undergoing any treatment that may involve essential oils, like a massage, as a few of these products could make symptoms worse. A health care provider can provide advice on suitable products.

Psoriasis will involve flares when symptoms worsen, and occasions of remission, whenever a person may not have any symptoms. Avoiding triggers, where possible, can help prevent a flare. Common triggers include:

- Stress

- Smoking

- Skin injury, including cuts, scrapes, and sunburn

- Sure medications, including some drugs for high blood circulation pressure, psychiatric disorders, arthritis, and malaria

- Infections and illnesses, such as strep throat, colds, and other common conditions

Triggers vary between individuals. Individuals who can identify their triggers should think it is easier to prevent them.

Medical therapy

Many different treatments are for sale to Psoriasis, and medical advances are producing treatment plans which may be far better than those obtainable in the past. The primary types of treatment that exist are:

- Biologics that are proving effective for moderate-to-severe symptoms

- Systemic, which affect the complete body

- Phototherapy, a kind of light treatment that folks can have within a doctor's office

- Fresh oral treatments, which prevent inflammation by inhibiting specific molecules

- Topical treatments for deciding on the skin

Discovering the right option requires guidance from a medical expert, who'll also discuss any home cures that might help.

CHAPTER 5

Psoriasis Dos and Don'ts

Whether you're simply starting psoriasis treatment or want far better therapies for your symptoms, you should strictly keep these important actions in mind.

If you're coping with Psoriasis, you certainly know how frustrating and challenging it could sometimes be to handle the problem. Symptoms like itchy, scaling skin make a restriction in your capability to perform day to day activities, have a toll on your psychological health, and impact yourself.

The good thing: You will find methods to make life with Psoriasis easier. Adopt these dos and don'ts to help get the symptoms in order greatly.

Psoriasis Dos

Do speak to a dermatologist. Schedule an appointment with a dermatologist who specializes in treating Psoriasis - she or he will be familiar with the most recent developments regarding treatment plans. Anticipate discussing the facts of your trouble with your doctor, including when you initially noticed it, what your symptoms are, any situations that appear to get your symptoms worse, and what treatments you have undergo and also have not worked for you personally before.

Do moisturize. Dry skin is more vulnerable to outbreaks of Psoriasis, so ensure that your skin is well lubricated. After bathing or showering, seal in moisture through the use of a generous amount of moisturizing cream or ointment to your skin layer. Vaseline, Cetaphil cream, and Eucerin cream certainly are a few commonly available moisturizers reported to supply great results. Avoid lightweight lotions, which don't contain enough emollients. If over-the-counter products don't help, your physician may prescribe a moisturizing cream that has medication.

Through the winter season it occur that everywhere do end up being moisturize, when cold weather and overheated buildings are drying combination. "In psoriasis, the skin accumulates rapidly, creating a thick scale," says James W. Swan, MD, professor of medicine in the division of dermatology at Loyola University infirmary in La Grange Park, Illinois.

When your skin is hydrated, the scales soften and fall away, alleviating itch and dryness. "However, not using anything on your skin for three days allows the skin to be very thick," says Dr. Swan.

Do have a soak. Soaking inside a warm (not hot) bath for a quarter-hour might help loosen scales and lessen the itching and inflammation due to Psoriasis. Adding sea salt, oatmeal, bath oil, or a bath gel containing coal tar towards the drinking water can further soothe and moisturize your skin layer. If you live within a region with mineral or salt baths, have it while bathing. Both are connected with relieving Psoriasis.

Do get some good sun. For factors experts still don't grasp, psoriasis lesions often diminish when subjected to ultraviolet light. So while sunbathing is discouraged for many people because of the chance of skin cancer, it could be helpful for people that have Psoriasis. The secret is to make sure that the areas suffering from Psoriasis are exposed.

Encompass unaffected skin with clothing or sunscreen with an SPF (sun protection factor) of at least 30. Limit sun contact with 15 minutes, and be careful to avoid sunburn, which may only help to make matters worse. It might take several weeks to find out a noticeable difference. Avoid tanning beds, which don't produce the same healing effect and could be harmful.

Your doctor could also recommend ultraviolet light therapy, either in the doctor's office or at home. According to Swan, "Among the gold standards for the treatment of psoriasis is phototherapy," that involves exposing your skin to ultraviolet light frequently and under medical supervision. Based on the National

Psoriasis Foundation, UVB light penetrates explicitly your skin and slows the growth of affected skin cells.

"Ultraviolet B (UVB) light reduces the inflammatory cells from your skin that's causing psoriasis," says Swan. "Also, it slows the cell proliferation that leads to scaling."

Do touch base. Having Psoriasis isn't only physically tough - it could be difficult emotionally as well. Feelings of depression, frustration, and isolation are normal. Body image issues linked to the looks of psoriasis lesions are normal. Although you may feel like you're the only person fighting this condition, actually, the World Health Organization reports that at least 100 million people are affected worldwide.

Discuss your feelings about the condition with your family, friends, and doctor. In-person and online organizations for all those with Psoriasis may also provide help and support you understand that you are not alone. Psoriasis organizations, like the National Psoriasis Foundation, can connect you with other people who live with Psoriasis, as well as preserve, you informed about research developments and opportunities to try fundraising walks and other events.

Psoriasis Don'ts

Don't overdo it. The ultimate way to handle Psoriasis is definitely to take action gently. Steer clear of the temptation to scratch or scrub lesions that will solely irritate them, producing them worse. Do not pick at scales that may cause bleeding and boost your threat of infection. Instead, talk to your physician about ointments and creams that can softly take away the thick scale. Bathing in scorching drinking water or using abrasive cleaners may also generate your symptoms flare up.

Don't stress out. Some individuals with Psoriasis state their condition worsens when they're under stress. Avoid stressful situations when you're able to, and take additional steps to deal with yourself - such as, eating well, exercise, and obtaining enough sleep - when you can't avoid stress. Hypnosis, relaxation, meditation, biofeedback, and other stress management techniques also may help.

Don't ignore flare-ups. Psoriasis can be a lifelong condition and one which will wax and wane as time passes. But it doesn't mean you need to live with it. In case your Psoriasis returns over time of being in order, schedule a visit with your doctor to learn and to decide what you can do to take care of it.

Don't quit. Probably one of the most frustrating reasons for having treating Psoriasis is that a thing that works well for just one person might not just work at all for another. It might take some time to get the correct therapy or mix of therapies that are most effective for you personally. Exercise patience, and don't quit. It is important to keep with your treatment solution, daytime in and day trip, even though your symptoms aren't so very bad. With Psoriasis, slow and steady wins the race.

CHAPTER 6

7 Methods for Psoriasis Skin Care

The itchy, inflamed skin that is included with Psoriasis is treatable. Producing simple tweaks to your day to day routine can promote healing and calm flare-ups.

1. Keep Your Skin Layer Moist

It's probably one of the most effective yet easiest actions you can take for irritated skin. It can help your skin layer, heal, and reduce dryness, itching, redness, soreness, and scaling.

Select your moisturizer predicated on how dry your skin layer is. Ointments are thick, heavy, and proficient at locking in moisture. Lotions are thinner and get absorbed easier. Or, you can select a cream. Remember, something doesn't need to be expensive to work effectively. Choose a fragrance-free moisturizer.

After your bath or shower is an excellent time for you to pat around the lotion gently. Reapply during the day so when you change clothes. Use more on cold or dry days.

Another way to keep your skin layer moist is by using a humidifier in your house, especially when the environment is usually hot and dry. If there is always heat, start the humidifier. It can help your skin layer retain moisture better.

2. Soothe With Warm Baths

A regular warm bath utilizing a mild soap might help soothe itchy places and remove dry skin.

Take quarter-hour to soak in the tepid to warm water. You will probably find comfort if you bring oil, finely ground oatmeal, Epsom salt, or the Dead Sea salt to your bath, but keep the drinking water and soap mild carefully. Hot temperatures and harsh soaps could be hard on the skin that's sensitive already.

Do not rub your skin layer using the towel as you dry off. Gently pat dry instead. The rubbing action could make sores worse as well as cause new ones. Unless you have time for any bath, you can nonetheless put a wet towel or cold compress on the difficult spot. You are learning much more about skincare methods for Psoriasis.

3. Heal With Sunlight

The ultraviolet (UV) light in sunlight can slow the growth of skin cells, so small exposure to the sun could be a great way to soothe, improve, as well as heal psoriasis lesions. Even indoor light could make a difference.

84

Try to get some good sun several times weekly and using sunscreen on your healthy skin. An excessive amount of sun (or sunburn) raises your threat of skin cancer and could make your outbreaks worse. Speak to your doctor before adding UV therapy to your routine. And schedule regular skin checkups to be sure you're not overcooking it.

4. Consider It Easy

Studies also show that stress could make Psoriasis and itching worse. Some individuals trace their first outbreak to an extremely stressful event. You may be in a position to calm symptoms by just cutting your anxiety.

There are numerous methods to lower stress. Create a support system of relatives and buddies. Consider what's most significant for you and devote some time to this: yoga, meditation, and yoga breathing help. A pleasant long walk around a nearby might calm you. Different ways to bust stress:

- Eat healthily.

- Drink a lot of water.

- Exercise regularly.

- Get a lot of sleep.

These may also assist you in fighting off infections that may trigger flares. See how to get psychological support during psoriasis treatment.

5. Proceed Easy on Yourself

Avoid severe products like lotions with alcohol, deodorant soaps, acids (glycolic, salicylic, and lactic acid), as well as some laundry soaps. These can inflame your sensitive skin. Feel the texture from the fabric from the clothes you get. Get them soft and comfortable. Avoid wool and mohair. They can irritate already inflamed skin.

6. Do not Scratch and Pick

There is no doubt about any of it: Whenever you get itch, your intention is to scratch. But scratching can rip off your skin layer, exposing your skin to infection-causing germs. It could also make sores appear where there weren't before. Keep the nails short and take an antihistamine if you're itchy.

And picking at your skin layer can result in infection. When you have an urge, close your eyes, breathe deeply, and gently rub on moisturizer instead.

7. Give Up Smoking And Limit Alcohol

Smoking can trigger flares. Speak to your doctor to assist

you to decide the ultimate way to quit. For a few, nicotine patches make Psoriasis worse.

Heavy drinking may also trigger symptoms. It could be dangerous when coupled with some psoriasis drugs. If you drink, keep it moderate -- that's up to at least one drink each day for ladies or 2 for men.

CHAPTER 7

Risks of Not Treating Psoriasis

Psoriasis is a chronic condition of the skin that triggers thick, red, scaly patches called plaques to build up. These plaques could be itchy, unpleasant, and embarrassing. For many individuals, having Psoriasis means you are not dealing with mere symptoms, but also with the treatments. Included in these are ointments and creams that may be messy, oral or injectable medications that may be expensive and involve severe risks and unwanted effects, and light treatments that may be inconvenient and time-consuming. And for most people, treatment or prevention of psoriasis flares is a life-long commitment.

You might wonder if it's worth all the trouble. And you'll

take into account the risks that include your psoriasis medications or treatments. However, the potential risks of not treating your Psoriasis are a lot more than skin deep.

Physical risks

Untreated Psoriasis can result in plaques that continue steadily to build and spread. These could be very painful, as well as the itching could be severe. Uncontrolled plaques may become infected and cause scars. Furthermore:

- Scalp psoriasis can result in hair loss, that could be permanent.

- You might develop painful adjustments in your nails, and you'll also lose your nails.

- When you have arthritis together with your Psoriasis (psoriatic arthritis), you could have joint pain, stiffness, and swelling. You need to consider oral or injectable medications because of this. If you don't treat this, you might have permanent joint damage, which may be unpleasant and disabling.

Increased frequency and severity of flares

Invest the daily medications to take care of and stop flares, not maintaining your treatments, could be exceptionally costly on your health. There's possibility for you to have more flares, combined with the pain and frustration that follows. And, stopping some medications suddenly or too early can result in the rebound effect. The rebound effect is when a flare occurs right after stopping treatment. Flares that occur with the rebound effect spread quickly and often have symptoms that are much worse than you are used to with typical flares.

Rarely, if you're not controlling your Psoriasis or stop your medications prematurely, you may also get a different kind of Psoriasis than the very one you are used to. Erythrodermic Psoriasis can be one type that can develop in people whose plaque psoriasis is uncontrolled. It is characterize by a severe, widespread, sunburn-like rash that leads to the peeling of the skin. People with this type of Psoriasis usually have severe itching and pain. They may develop swelling, infections, or congestive heart failure. Many people with this form of Psoriasis need to be treated in the hospital, and a few may even die from complications.

Reduced standard of living

The pain and itching that go with psoriasis flares will keep you up during the night and make you feel tired the very next day. This may affect how you do at your task or in school. Severe psoriasis symptoms could make it difficult for you to take good care of yourself or your family. Psoriasis of your hands or feet can interfere with your ability to do your job, play sports, or engage in hobbies. You may even have trouble walking and keep yourself active. Many people with Psoriasis feel unattractive and isolate themselves from others. They may avoid going out in public, wearing clothing that shows their plaques, or participating in activities like swimming that make it difficult to hide their symptoms. Experts find that people who can control their psoriasis report a higher quality of life, miss less work, and are more productive at work.

Depression, anxiety, and suicide

Stress could be a trigger and a consequence of psoriasis flares. People who have Psoriasis have an increased threat of depression and anxiety than those without it. There are also more suicidal thoughts and attempts, particularly if their disease is severe. The social isolation that often goes along with having Psoriasis could make depression symptoms worse. Fortunately, studies show that treating your Psoriasis can improve symptoms of depression.

Various other inflammatory conditions

Psoriasis can be an inflammatory disease. People who have Psoriasis will have some other inflammatory conditions such as coronary attack, stroke, type 2 diabetes, and inflammatory bowel disease. This is also true for those who have severe Psoriasis. Researchers aren't sure if having Psoriasis causes these conditions or if shared factors related to them. However, maintaining your Psoriasis in order may decrease your risks. Based on the National Psoriasis Foundation, treating your Psoriasis has been shown to reduce your risk of heart attack and stroke.

Not only skin deep

As you can see, treating your Psoriasis is approximately much more than merely treating your skin layer. Getting the Psoriasis in order, and keeping it in order, can greatly help to improve yourself and lessen your risks of physical, emotional, as well as life-threatening complications. Work closely together with your doctor to discover a treatment solution that meets your goals and fits your way of life. And, commit to staying on track for life.

Acknowledgments

The Glory of this book success goes to God Almighty and my beautiful Family, Fans, Readers & well-wishers, Customers and Friends for their endless support and encouragements.